1 A Crab Goes for a Walk

■Draw a line from one crab (🦀) to the other crab (🦀).

To parents
Here the exercise is to draw straight lines vertically and horizontally. Do the exercise along with your child if he or she has difficulty.

■Draw a line from one picture to the matching picture.

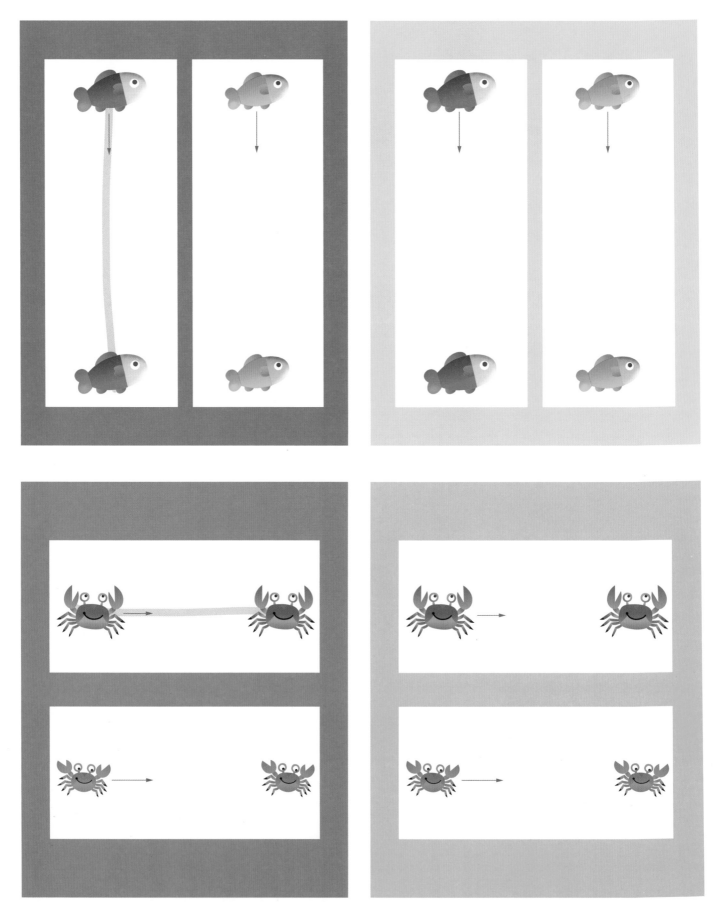

2

2 In the Woods

Name

Date

To parents Have your child draw a line from one rabbit to the other rabbit. Your child may draw the line however he or she likes. You may give your child hints. For example, "Don't let the rabbit run into a stump!"

■ Draw a line from one rabbit ( ) to the other rabbit ( ).

3

■Draw a line from one picture to the matching picture.

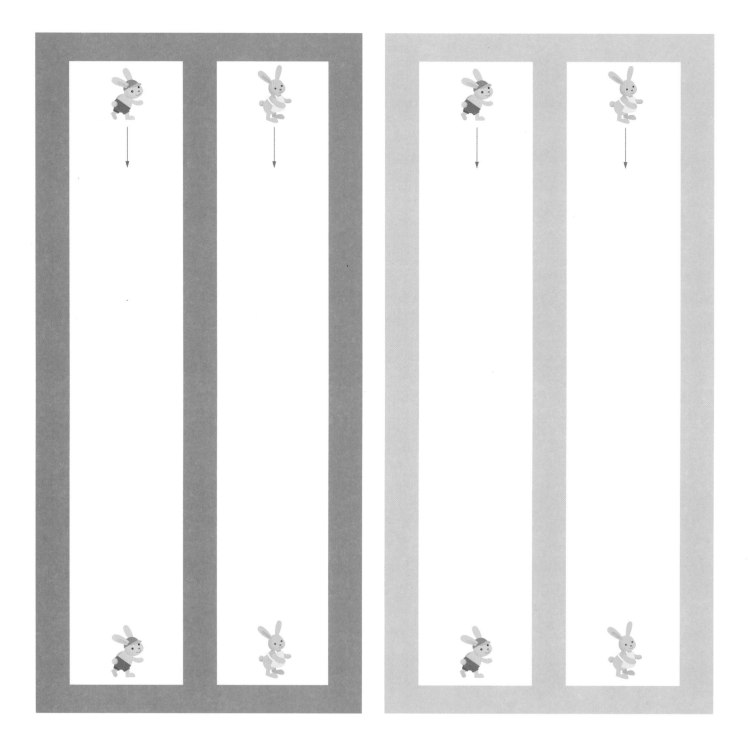

To parents Have your child draw a line from one cat to the other cat. Your child may draw the line however he or she likes. You may give your child hints. For example, "The cat should stay out of the holes and puddles!"

■Draw a line from one cat () to the other cat ( ).

■Draw a line from one picture to the matching picture.

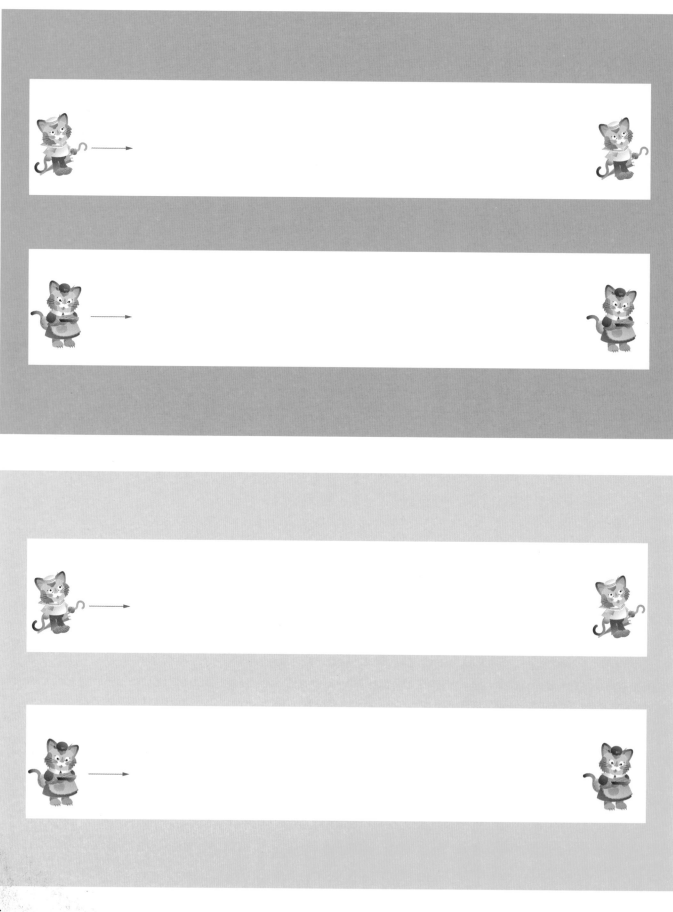

4 A Race in the Swimming Pool

Name

Date

To parents The exercise here is to draw straight lines, even if they go outside the area. Have your child draw lines slowly and carefully.

■Draw a line from one boy (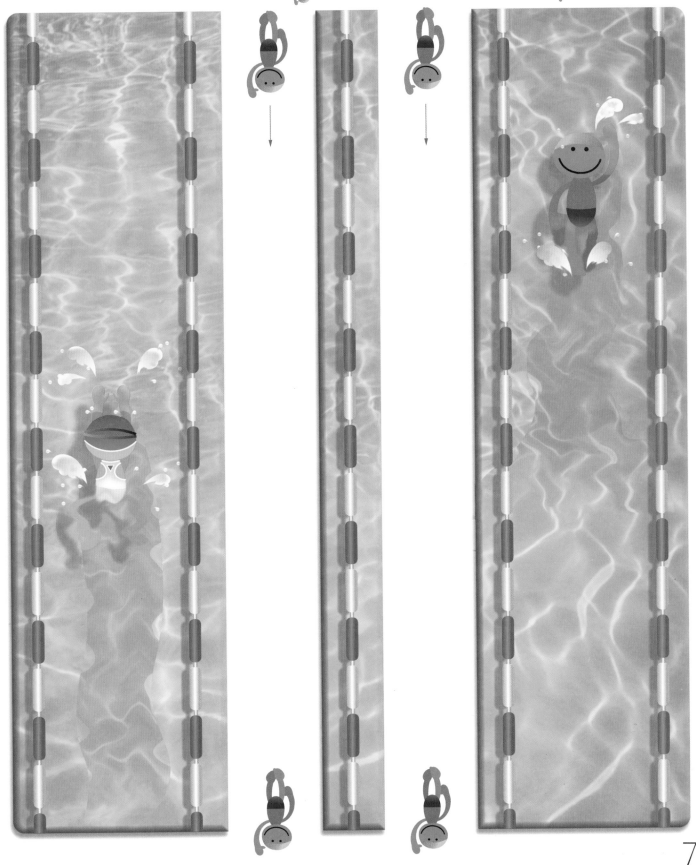) to the matching boy ( ).

■Draw a line from one picture to the matching picture.

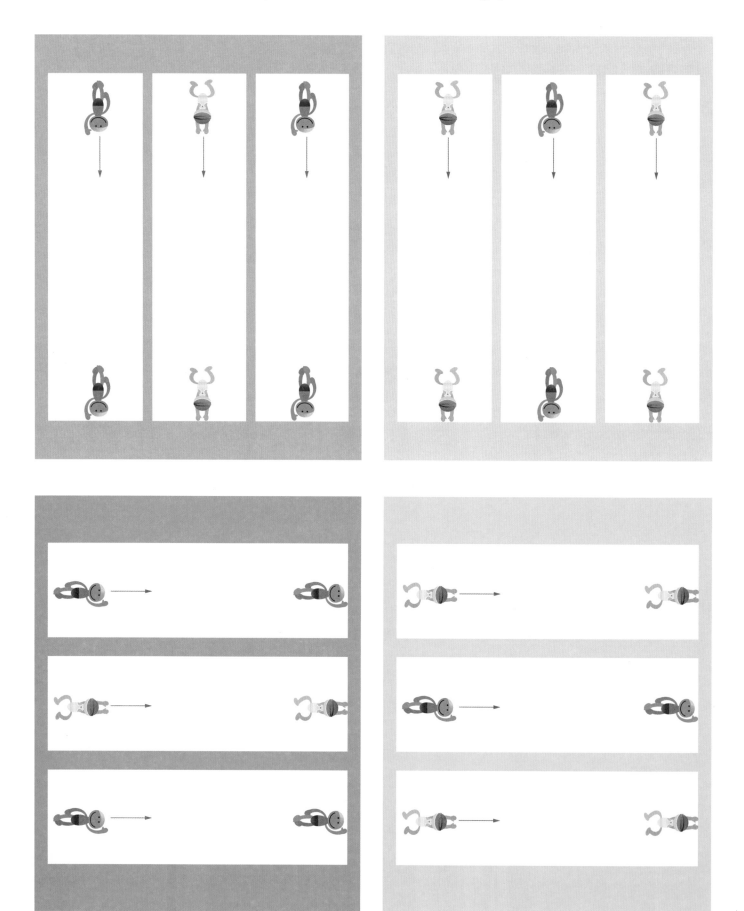

8

Sea Creatures

Name

Date

To parents
If drawing a diagonal line in one stroke is too difficult, your child may pause in the middle.

■Draw a line from one shell ( ) to the matching shell ( ).

■Draw a line from one picture to the matching picture.

6 A Bear Paints a Barn

Name

Date

To parents This exercise teaches your child to draw jagged lines. This is often very difficult for children. To make this activity easier, allow your child to draw a straight line to the middle brush, then continue drawing to the brush at the bottom.

■ Draw a line from one brush (🖌) to the matching brush (🖌).

To parents

Encourage your child to draw a jagged line from start to finish in one stroke. If your child needs help, allow your child to draw a straight line to the middle picture, then continue drawing to the end of the picture.

■Draw a line from one picture to the matching picture.

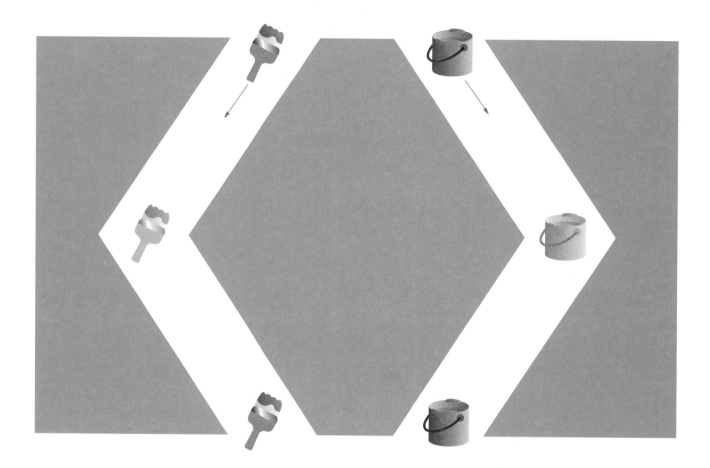

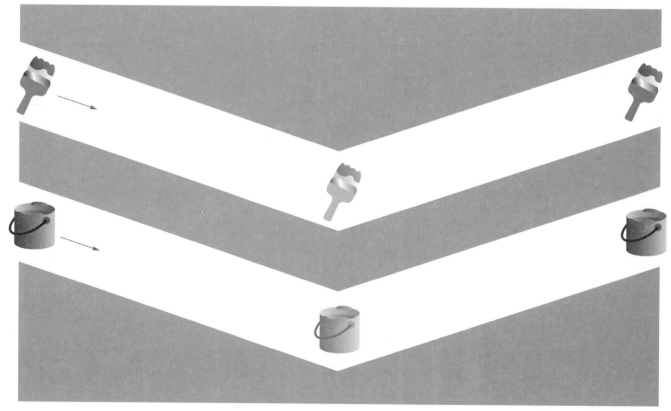

Flying Over the Rainbow

Name

Date

To parents This exercise teaches your child to draw curved lines. Have your child move the pencil slowly along the curved path.

■ Draw a line from one paper plane () to the matching paper plane ( ).

To parents
Encourage your child to draw curved lines, showing the path of the paper planes.

■Draw a line from one picture to the matching picture.

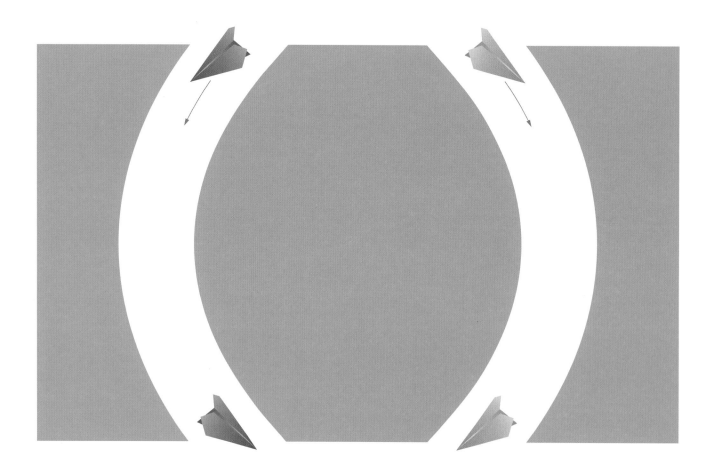

Swimming Freely in the Sea

Name

Date

■Draw a line from one dolphin () to the matching dolphin ( ).

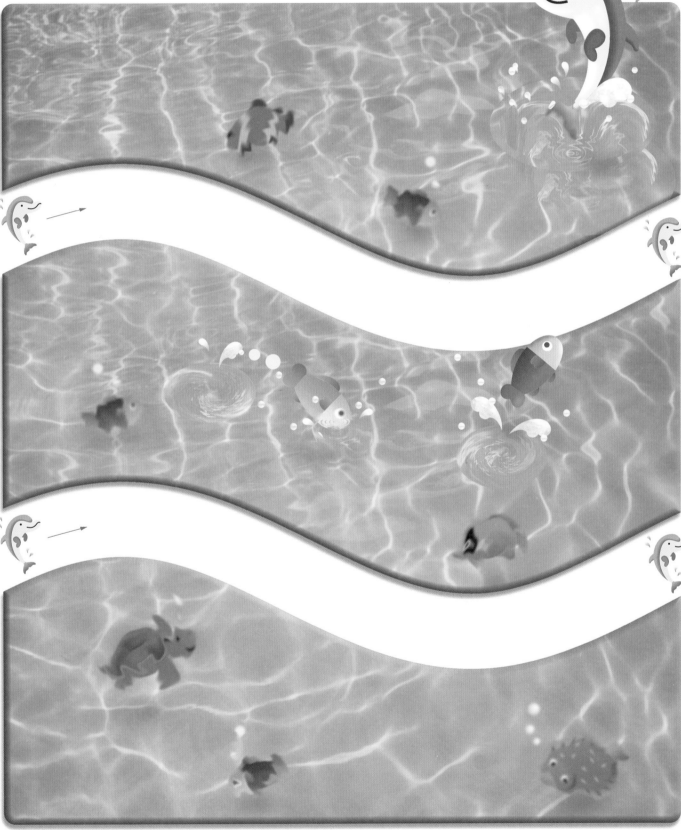

15

■Draw a line from one picture to the matching picture.

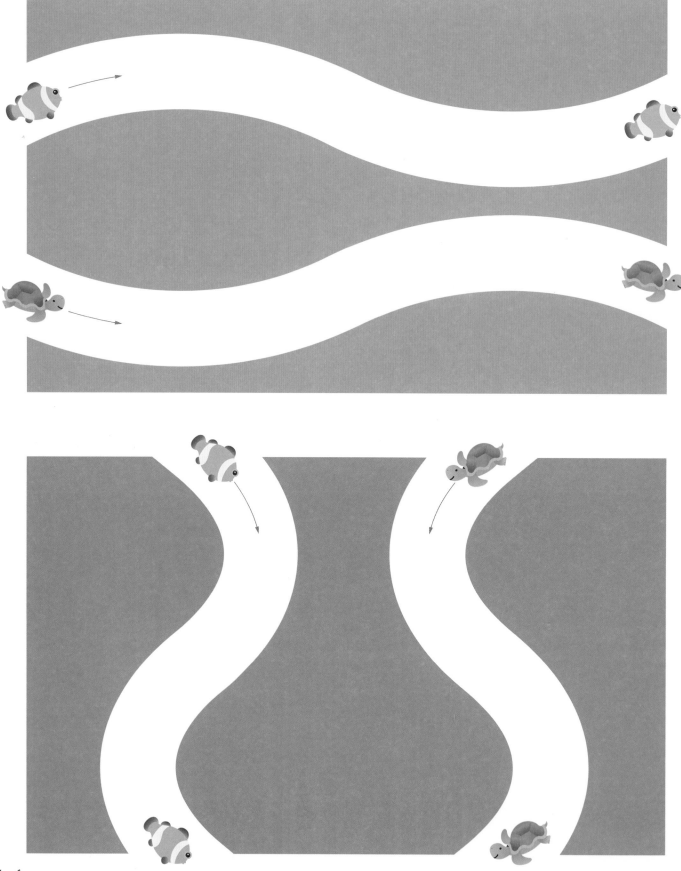

9 It's a Long Hit!

Name

Date

To parents From this page on, drawing lines becomes more difficult. It is all right if your child draws outside the area. The important thing is to encourage your child to draw slowly and carefully.

■Draw a line from one ball () to the other ball ( ).

To parents
This exercise teaches your child to draw curved lines. There may be round shapes—a ball, a balloon—around you. Drawing them too, along with your child, will greatly help his or her pencil-stroke practice.

■Draw a line from one picture to the matching picture.

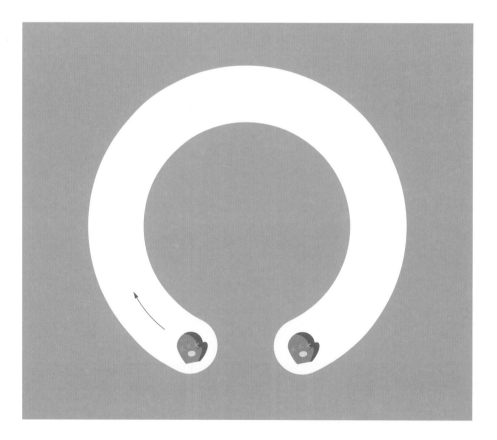

18

A Tour of the Zoo

■ Draw a line from one friend (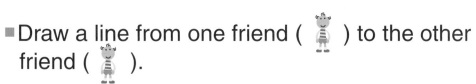) to the other
  friend ( ).

19

■Draw a line from one picture to the matching picture.

Name

Date

■Draw a line from one camel () to the other camel ( ).

To parents

On the following pages your child will learn to draw zigzag lines. This is often very difficult for children. To make this activity easier, allow your child to draw lines connecting one camel to the next camel, until your child has reached the end of the zigzag line.

■Draw a line from one picture to the matching picture.

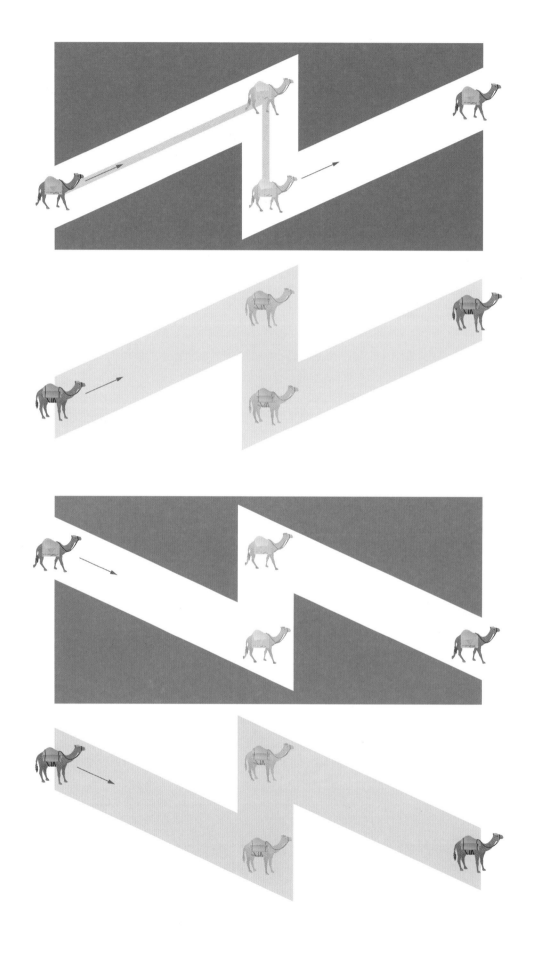

12 A Flash of Lightning

Name

Date

To parents
Drawing a zigzag line is very difficult for a child. To make this activity easier, allow your child to draw a straight line from one dog to the next dog, then continue on to the end.

■ Draw a line from one dog () to the other dog ( ).

23

To parents
Begin by having your child draw a line from one picture to the next. When he or she has gotten used to this, encourage your child to draw a zigzag line in one stroke.

■Draw a line from one picture to the matching picture.

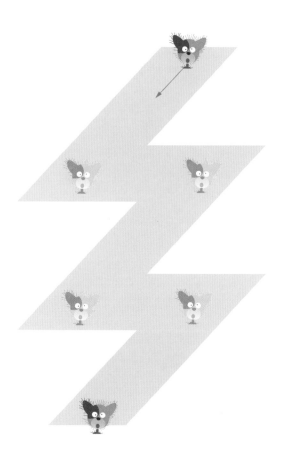

13 Seashore Swimming

■Draw a line from one boy (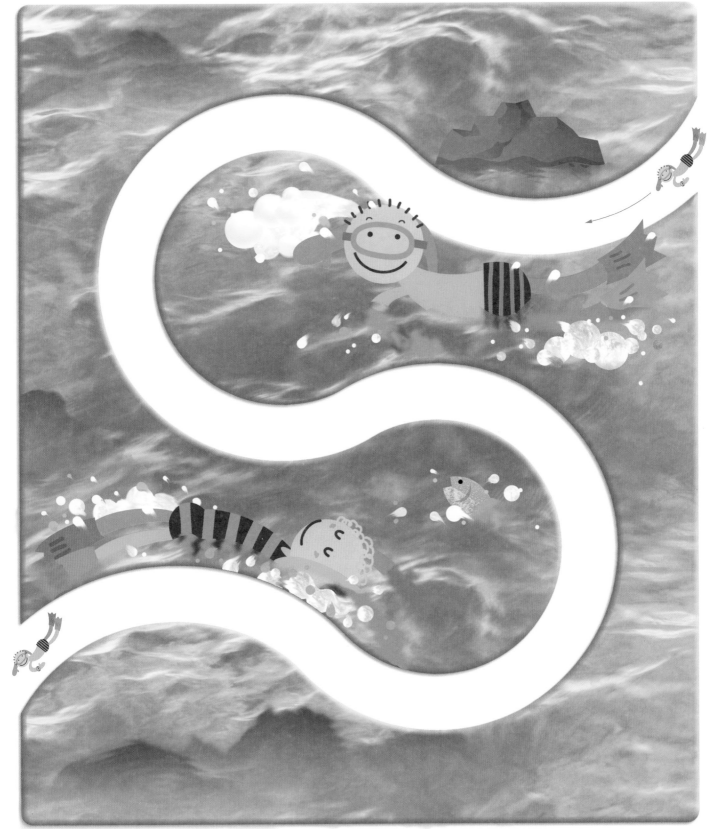) to the other boy ( ).

To parents
Encourage your child to draw a line from one swimmer to the other swimmer. Point at the start and at the end and tell your child, "Try to swim from here to there."

■Draw a line from one picture to the matching picture.

26

■Draw a line from one kayak () to the other kayak ( ).

■Draw a line from one picture to the matching picture.

15 Treasure Hunt

Name

Date

To parents From this page on, drawing lines becomes more difficult. It's okay if your child draws outside the area. The important thing is to encourage your child to draw slowly and carefully.

■ Draw a line from one treasure chest () to the other treasure chest ( ).

To parents
On pages 30, 32, 34, and 36, the exercise is to
draw a single line through all the pictures.

■Draw a line from the dot (●) to the star (★) through all the fruit.

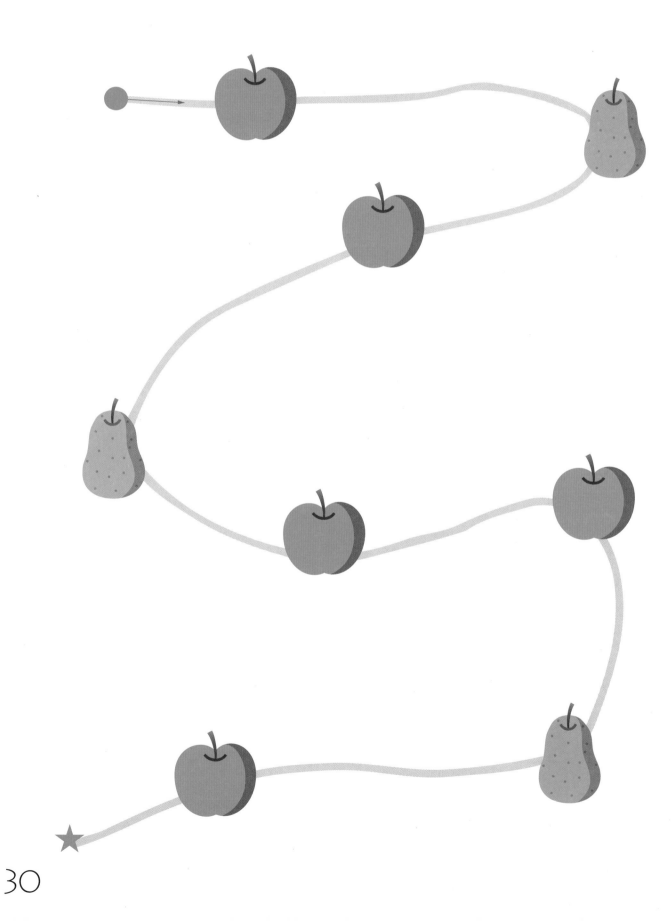

30

Name

Date

■Draw a line from one ant () to the other ant ( ).

31

■Draw a line from the dot (●) to the star (★) through all the cars.

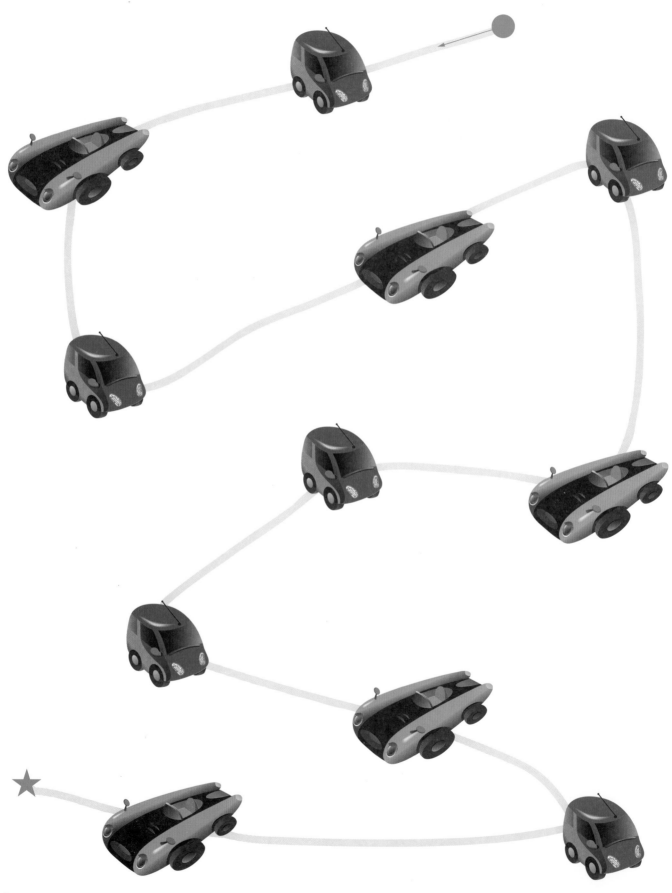

In the Park

Name

Date

■Draw a line from one ball (⚽) to the other ball (⚽).

33

To parents
On pages 34 and 36, no example line is shown. It is all right to go in any order and pass through the same point several times.

■Draw a line from the dot (●) to the star (★) through all the cups and glasses.

34

■Draw a line from one ball () to the other ball ( ).

■Draw a line from the dot (●) to the star (★) through all the butterflies and bees.

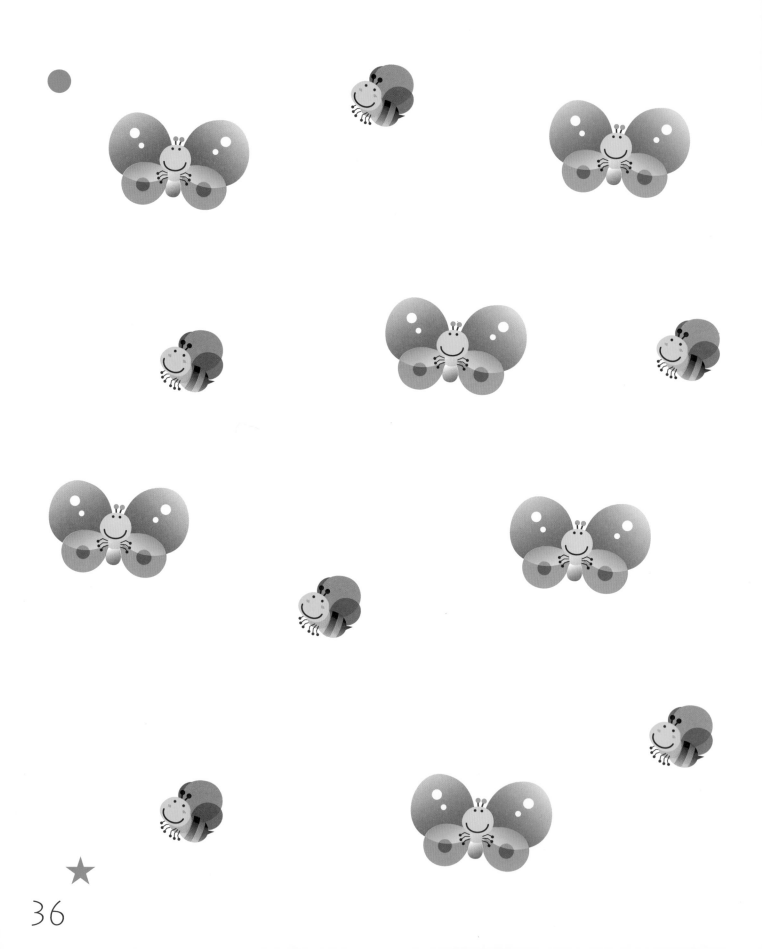

36

■Draw a line from one car ( ) to the other car ( ).

To parents
Have your child draw a steady line from the dot to the star. When your child has finished, ask him or her what is shown in the picture. Color the picture for some extra fun!

■Draw a line from the dot (●) to the star (★).

38

Seal

■Draw a line from one car (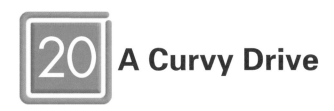) to the other car ( ).

39

To parents
Have your child draw a steady line from the dot to the star. When your child has finished, ask him or her what is shown in the picture. Color the picture for some extra fun!

■Draw a line from the dot (●) to the star (★).

40

Frog

21 Going Down a Snowy Mountain

■Draw a line from one sled ( ) to the other sled ( ).

To parents
Have your child draw a steady line from the dot to the star.
When your child has finished, ask him or her what is
shown in the picture. Color the picture for some extra fun!

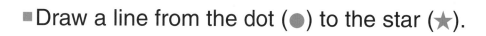

■Draw a line from the dot (●) to the star (★).

42

Snake

Dollhouse

■Draw a line from one doll ( ) to the other doll ( ).

43

■Draw a line from the dot (●) to the star (★).

44

Umbrella

23 Choo-Choo

To parents
Have your child draw the path of the steam engine. Make sure your child follows the arrows at the crossing point so that he or she draws a line in the right direction.

■ Draw a line from one steam engine (🚂) to the other steam engine (🚂).

To parents
It is very difficult for a child to bring a pencil to a dead stop at the end of the line. From this page on, have your child be careful to stop at the end (★). It helps to tell him or her, "Spin, spin, and stop!"

■Draw a line from the dot (●) to the star (★).

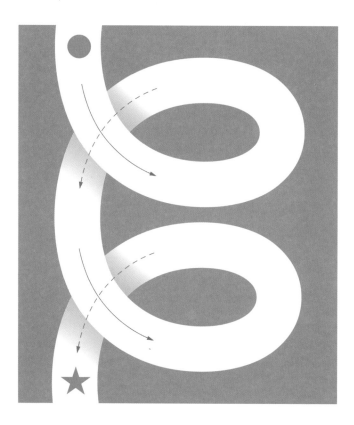

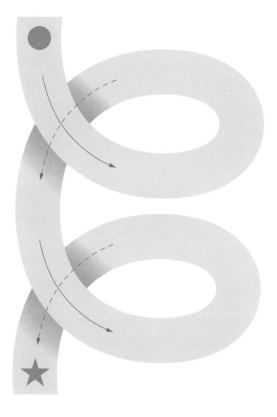

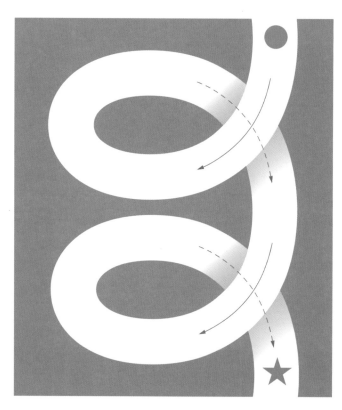

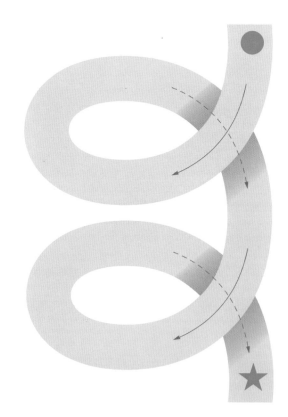

46

■Draw a line from one tiger () to the other tiger ( ).

■Draw a line from the dot (●) to the star (★).

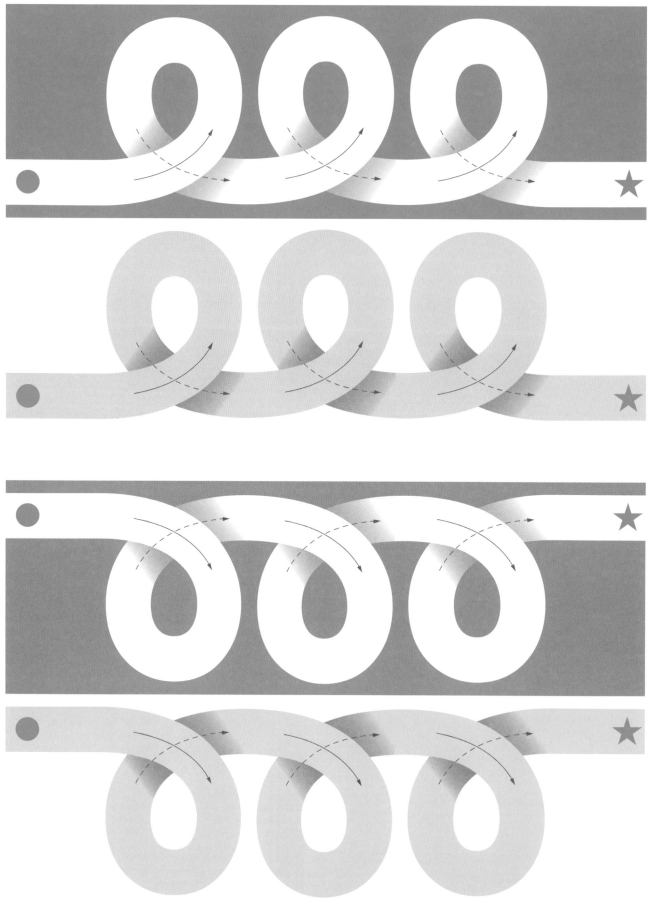

48

Water Slide

Name

Date

■Draw a line from one girl () to the other girl ( ).

■Draw a line from the dot (●) to the star (★).

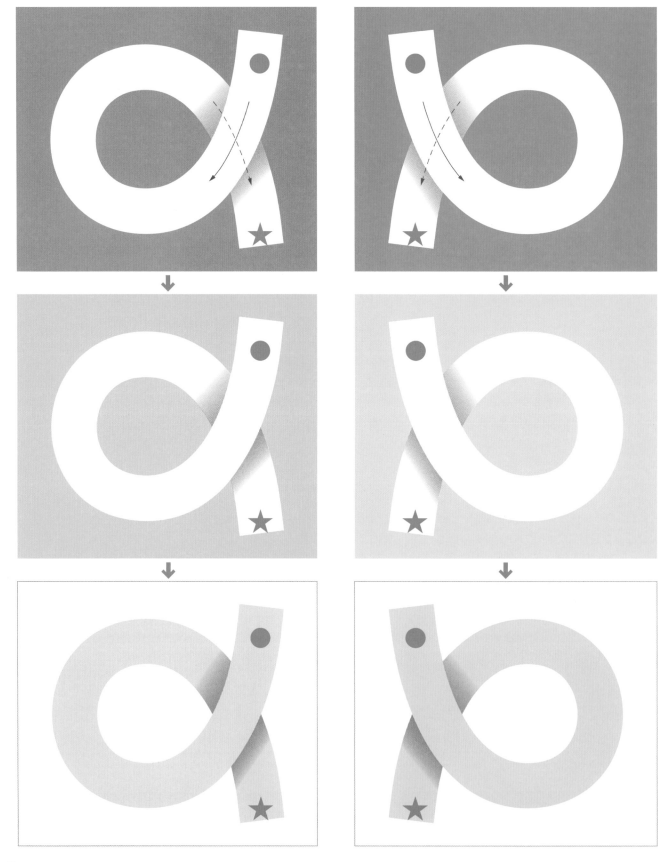

Name

Date

To parents
From this page on, drawing lines becomes more difficult. Encourage your child to draw within the lines. It is important for your child to develop the ability to draw carefully and steadily.

■Draw a line from one T-shirt () to the matching T-shirt ( ).

■Draw a line from the dot (●) to the star (★).

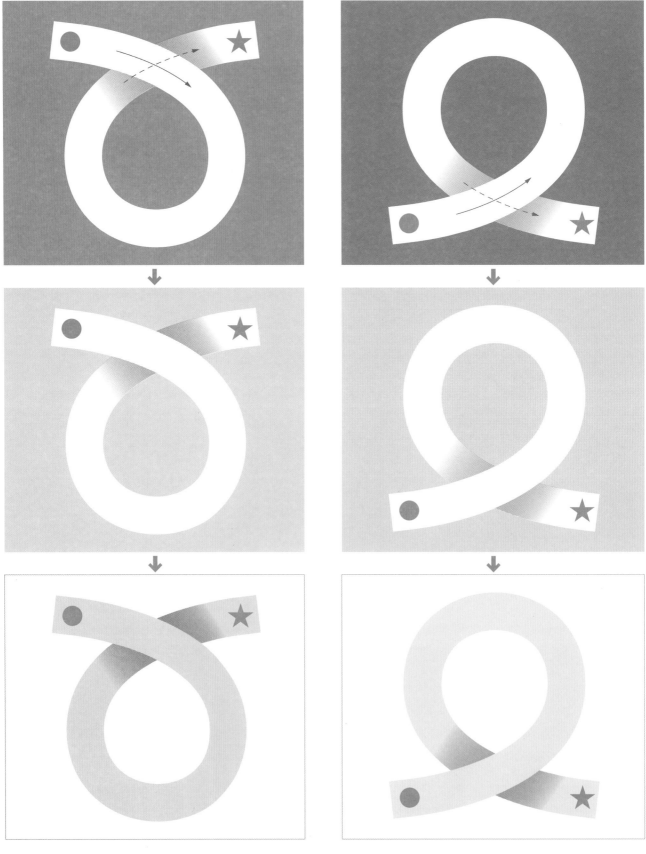

Which Book to Read?

■Draw a line from one book () to the matching book ().

To parents
This activity teaches your child to draw lines of two or more strokes. Have your child begin by drawing a line from the numeral 1 to the matching star, then drawing a line from the numeral 2 to the matching star.

■Draw a line in the red path (❶) and then the blue path (❷).

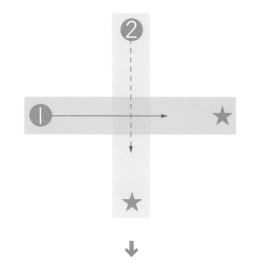

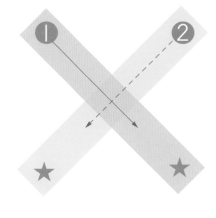

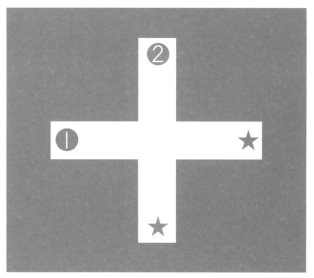

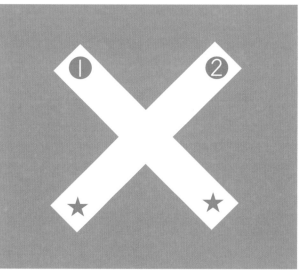

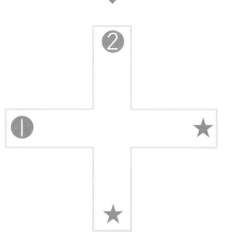

28

Magic Hands

Name

Date

■Draw a line from one piece of candy ()
to the matching piece of candy ( ).

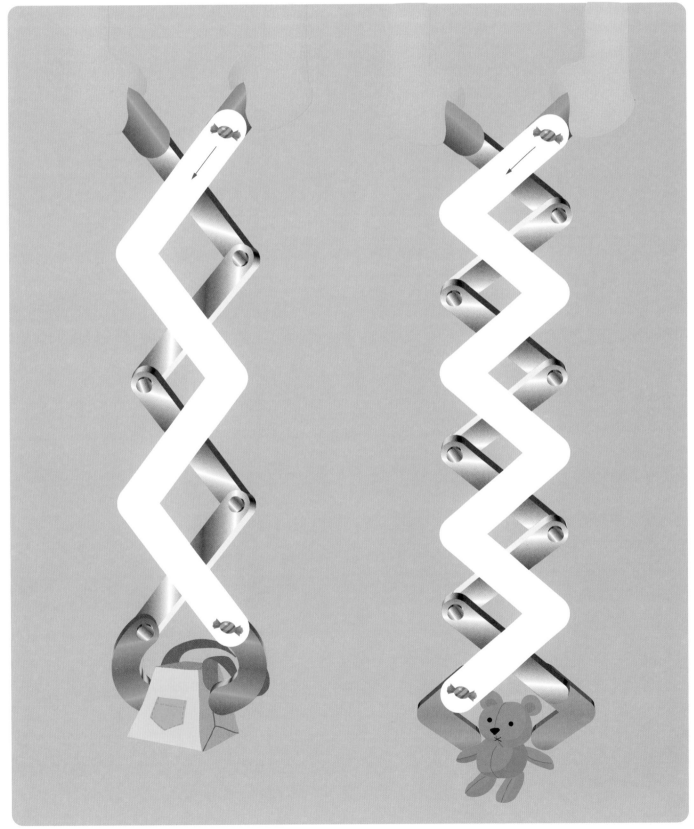

■Draw a line in the red path (❶) and then the blue path (❷).

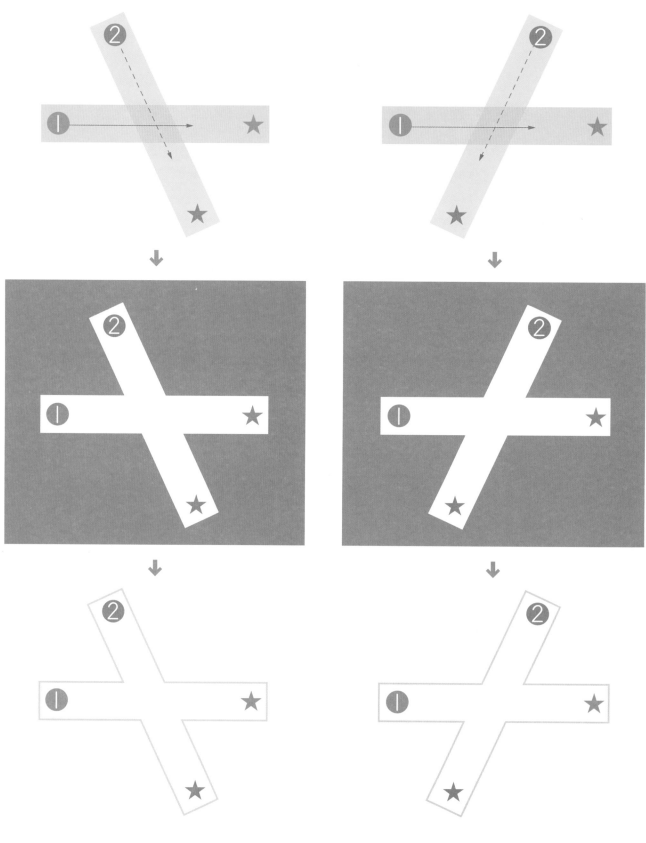

Exploring a Department Store

Name

Date

■Draw a line from one ball (🏀) to the other ball (🏀).

■Draw a line in the red path (❶) and then the blue path (❷).

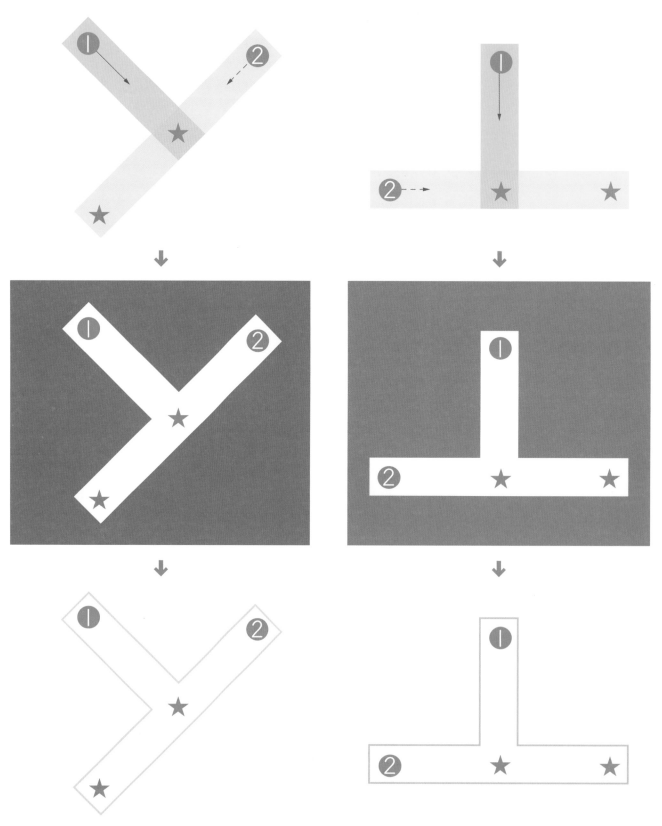

58

30 Space Flight

Name

Date

■Draw a line from one UFO (🛸) to the other UFO (🛸).

59

■Draw a line in the red path (**1**), then the blue (**2**), and then
the yellow path (**3**).

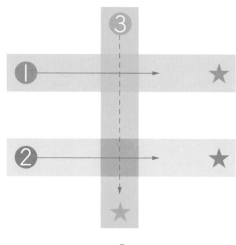

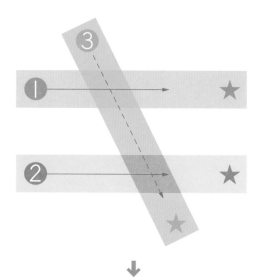

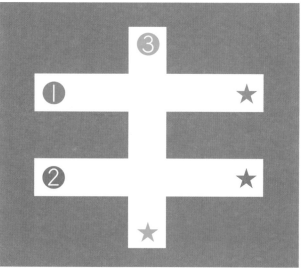

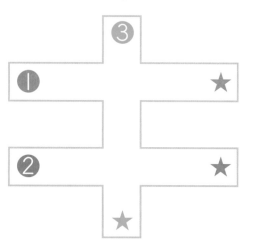

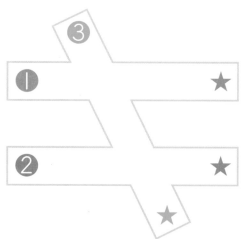

60

Scary Haunted House

Name

Date

■Draw a line from one ghost () to the other ghost ( ).

■Draw a line in the red path (❶), then the blue (❷), and then the yellow path (❸).

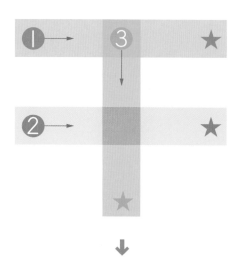

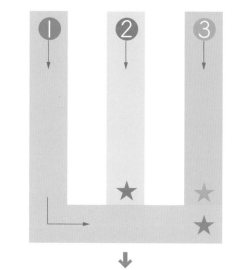

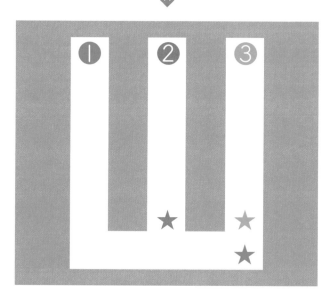

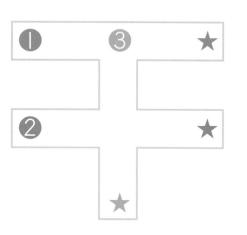

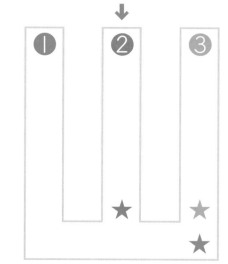

■Draw a line from one green caterpillar () to the other green caterpillar ( ).

■Draw a line from the dot (●) to the star (★).

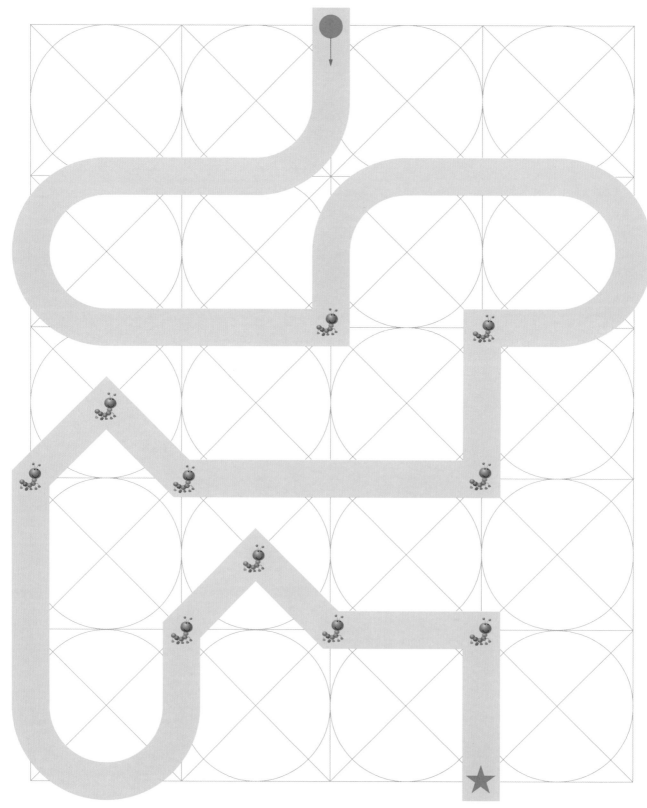

Surfing

To parents
At the crossing point, have your child follow the direction of the arrow. Encourage your child not to go outside of the area.

■Draw a line from one tiger ( ) to the other tiger ( ).

■Draw a line from the dot (●) to the star (★).

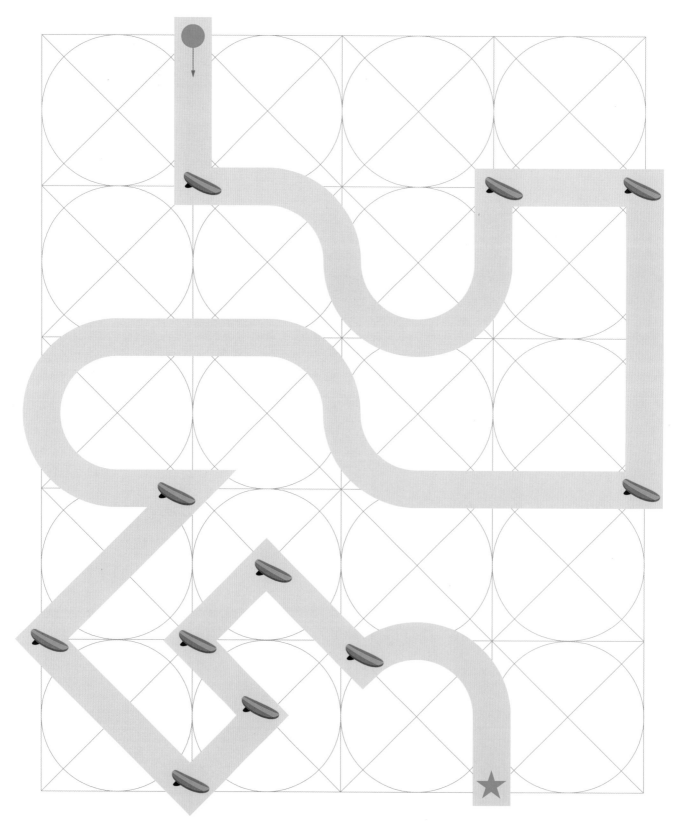

34 Doing Loop-the-Loops

To parents
From this page on, the paths are even narrower. It is more important that your child draw slowly and carefully than that he or she draw in one stroke.

■Draw a line from one balloon ( ) to the other balloon ( ).

■Draw a line from the dot (●) to the star (★).

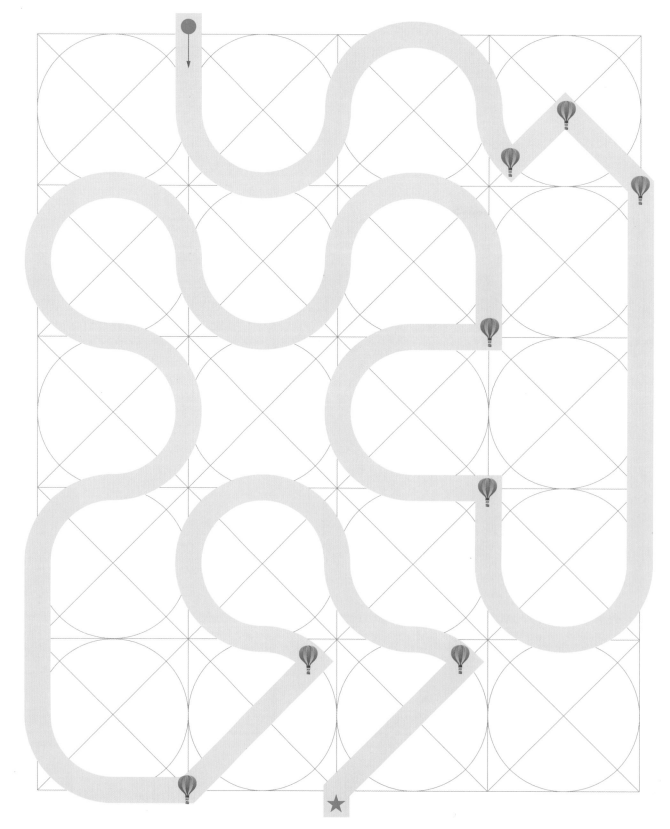

To parents
Encourage your child to use his or her experience drawing zigzag and curved lines to complete this activity.

■ Draw a line from one tiger () to the other tiger ( ).

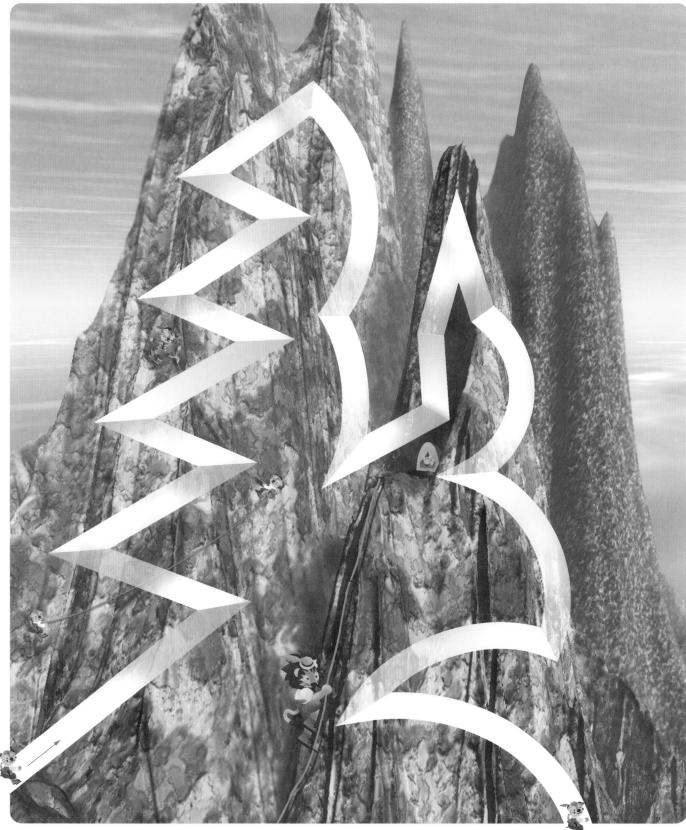

69

■Draw a line from the dot (●) to the star (★).

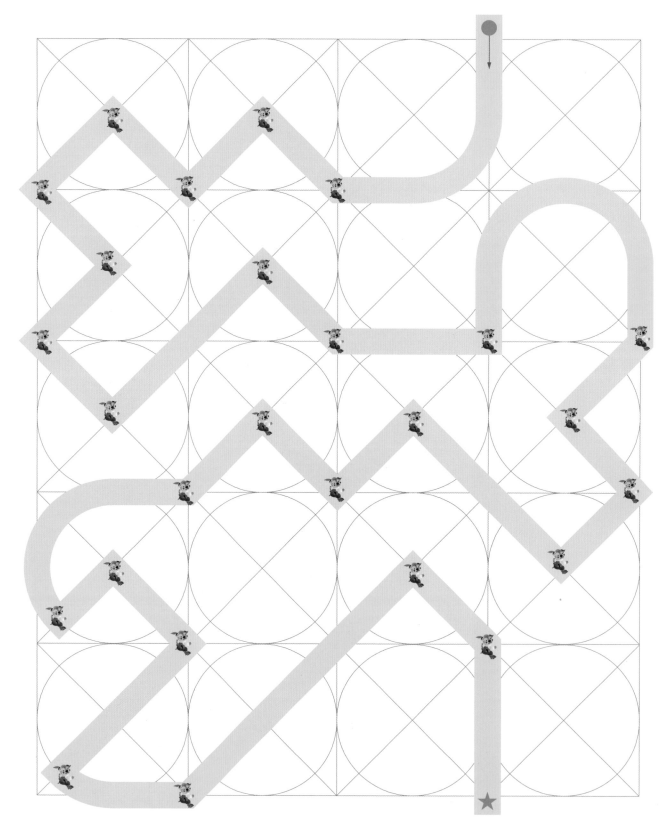

70

Name

Date

■Draw a line from one car (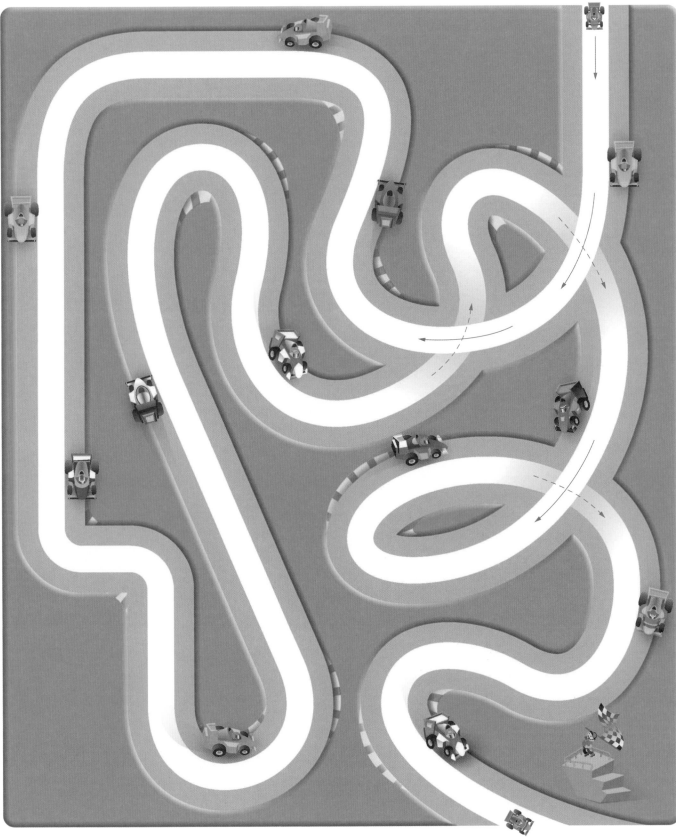) to the other car ( ).

■Draw a line from the dot (●) to the star (★).

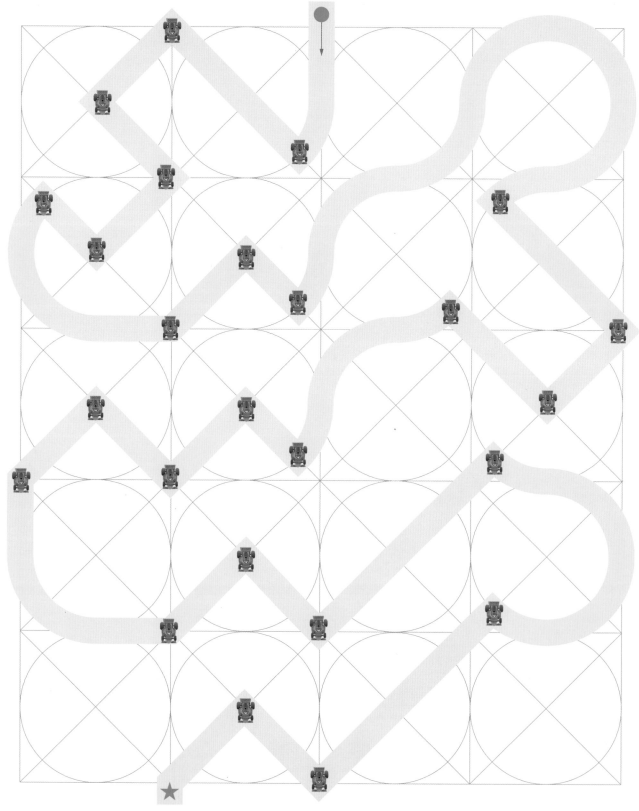

Name

Date

■ Draw a line from one girl () to the other girl ( ).

73

To parents
From this page on, drawing lines becomes more difficult. Encourage your child to draw within the lines. It is important for your child to develop the ability to draw carefully and steadily.

■Draw a line from the dot (●) to the star (★).

Racing Car

Name

Date

To parents Encourage your child to draw along very narrow paths. Make sure that your child can easily draw a steady line along the path.

■Draw a line from one coaster car ( ) to the other coaster car ( ).

■Draw a line from the dot (●) to the star (★).

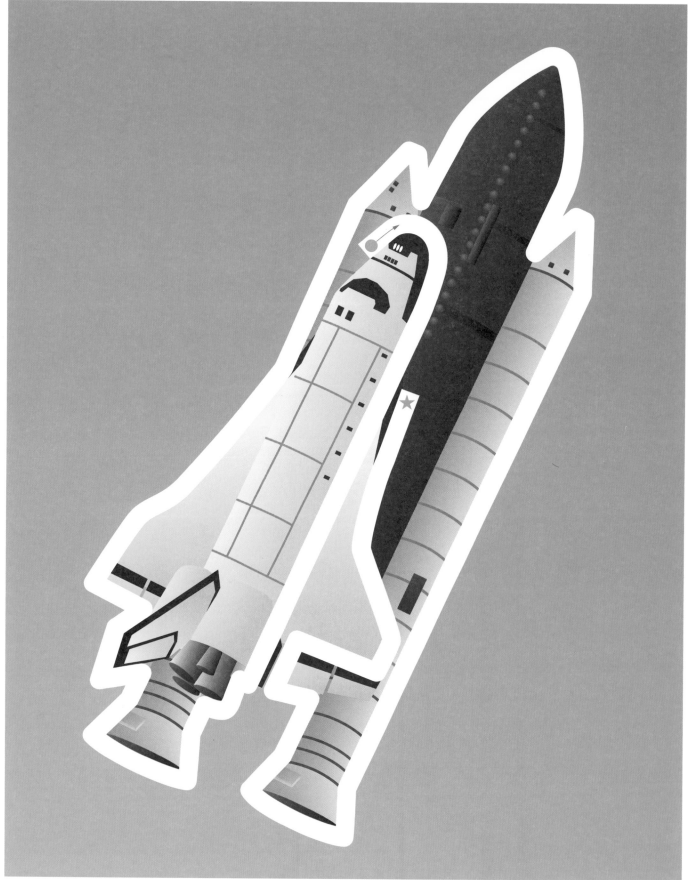

Space Shuttle

Mountainside Roller Coaster

Name

Date

■Draw a line from one coaster car () to the other coaster car ().

■Draw a line from the dot (●) to the star (★).

Sailboat

40 Roller Coaster in Space

Name

Date

■Draw a line from one coaster car ( ) to the other coaster car ( ).

79

To parents
Has your child had fun reaching the end of the book? By now he or she should be able to draw lines fairly well and with more confident strokes than on the first page. Give your child lots of praise for his or her effort!

■Draw a line from the dot (●) to the star (★).

Castle

KUMON

Certificate of Achievement

____

is hereby congratulated on completing

My First Book of Tracing

Presented on ______________________, 20____

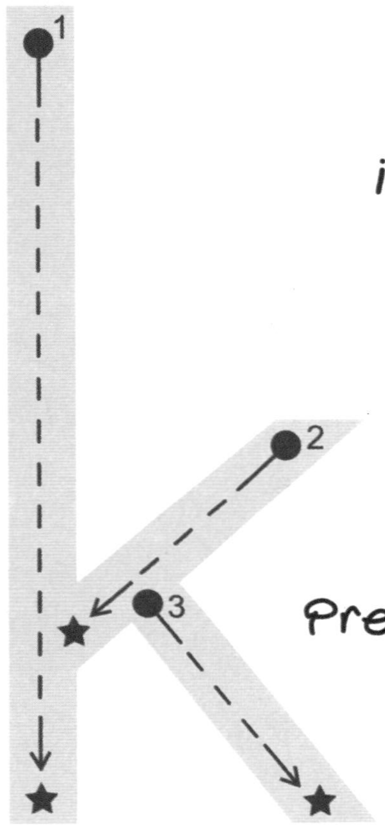

trace me

____

Parent or Guardian